AF440887

Shivohum
https://www.shutterstock.com/g/talkingclips
E-mail: talkingclips@yahoo.com; vkapoor1@yahoo.com
Tel: (+91 9810344412)

Meet the
Characters

Little Bee Boo

Boo's Mother
Dew

The bathing Butterfly

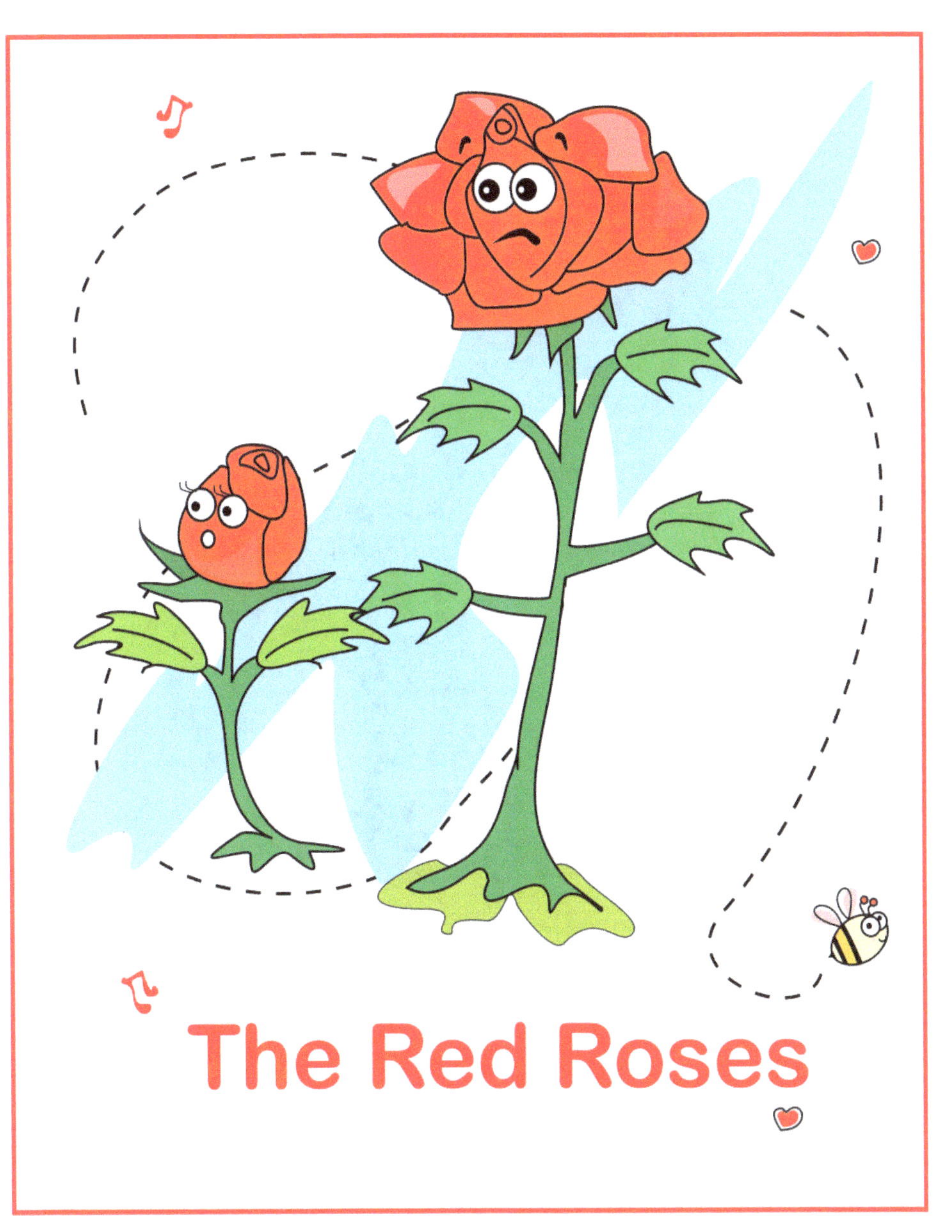

The Red Roses

The Kung-fu
Caterpillar

The Hop Hop Squirrel

The Fat Mouse

Little Bee Boo, has been worryingly flying all around the zoo on her birthday.
She's been asking the same question to everyone she meets.

What exactly has gone wrong?
Will Boo find a solution to her problem?

This story is about a little Bee named 'Boo'

and her new 'Blue Shoe'.

Baby Boo lived with her mother 'Dew' in the city Zoo.

They had a small hive

on a tall tree that was surrounded with lots of flowering plants.

It was Boo's birthday. As the morning sun rose,
sparkling rays came right through Boo's window to wake her up.
Boo had no idea how her birthday was going to unfold.
Let's peep through Boo's window and see how her day goes.

'Good morning sweetheart,
and a very happy birthday', whispered Dew.
'It's your first birthday, and you are 1 week old today.
Wake up quick, and see what I've brought for your present.'

'A PRESENT!' screamed Boo, as she jumped off her bed.
'Can I see it please? Please, please, please mom', she pleaded.
'Not now sweetie' said Dew smilingly. 'You need to get ready first.
I know for sure that when you see your gift,
you would want to fly out with it.'

Boo was very excited.
She quickly rushed to the bathroom, brushed her teeth,
took a shower, got all tidy, and swiftly flew out;

and then, she caught sight of her bed.

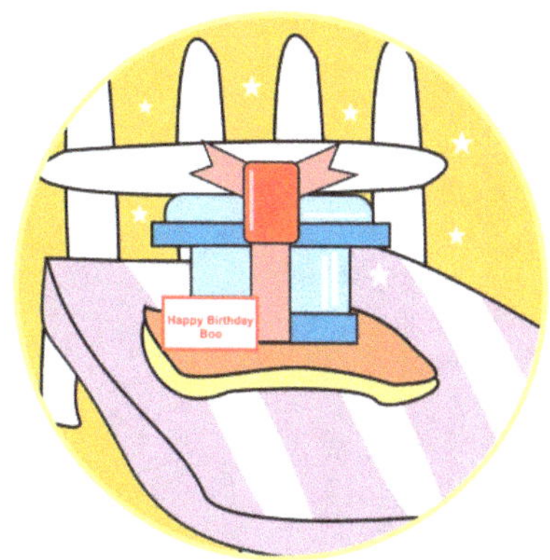

'**Wow!**' she whispered, as she looked at a shiny little box
placed on her pillow.
It was beautifully wrapped, and had a card placed next to it.
The card read – 'To the love of my life – Happy Birthday Boo'.

'Go on. Open It', said Dew, 'and see what I've got for you'.

Boo quickly flew towards her gift.
She started unwrapping the box;
and as it opened, her eyes gleamed
looking at the beautiful shiny gift
her mom had brought.

'Shoes!' she said excitedly. 'My first pair of shoes!'
'Thank you mom, for bringing me such a lovely gift.'
'Can I wear it now?' she requested.
'Of course my dear', said Dew. 'It's your birthday.
Go enjoy yourself outside and have fun. It's your day today'.

Boo quickly jumped into her new shoes.
They seemed a little big for her size,
but she was too excited to let that stop her
from wearing them for her next flight.

'Bye mom' she said, as she quickly flew out of the window
towards the open blue.

She flew up, and she flew down;
around the trees, and over the open grounds.
Baby Boo flew all over the zoo that day.

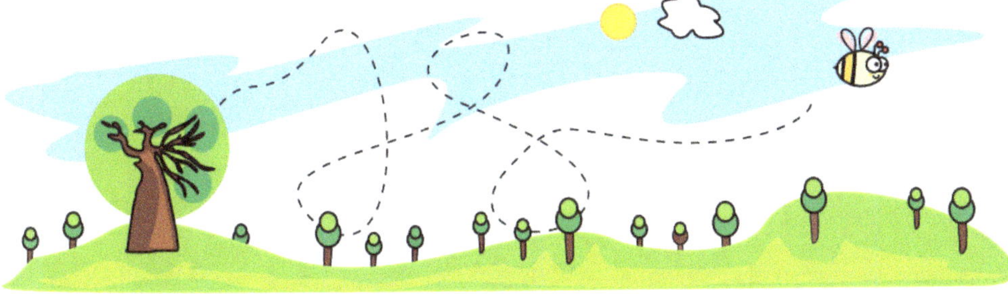

Then, suddenly, baby Boo stopped.
Something did not seem right.
Baby Boo looked up, and then she looked down.
She looked up again, and then slowly she looked down again.

This time when she looked down, she noticed something
that drained all her excitement instantly.

What exactly had happened? What did baby Boo see?
Let's find this out together.

Let the rhyme begin -

Her eyes were wet with tears coming through,
Away from home, and deep in the zoo,
Little baby Boo had 'Lost One Shoe'.
She looked all around as she flew, flew, flew.
But little baby Boo had lost her shoe.

Up above and under all across the zoo,
Little baby Boo could not find her shoe.

AND THEN?

BOO, BOO, BOO,
cried little baby Boo,
BOO, BOO, BOO,
'I lost my shoe!'.

Boo came close to the Butterfly, and asked-
Hello Mr. Butterfly, how are you?
I am Boo, and I lost my Shoe.

The Butterfly looked at Boo, and said-
Oh! little Boo, I see that too,
You've lost one of the two, two, two.
Check with the Roses I heard they overgrew,
They might be wearing your little blue shoe.

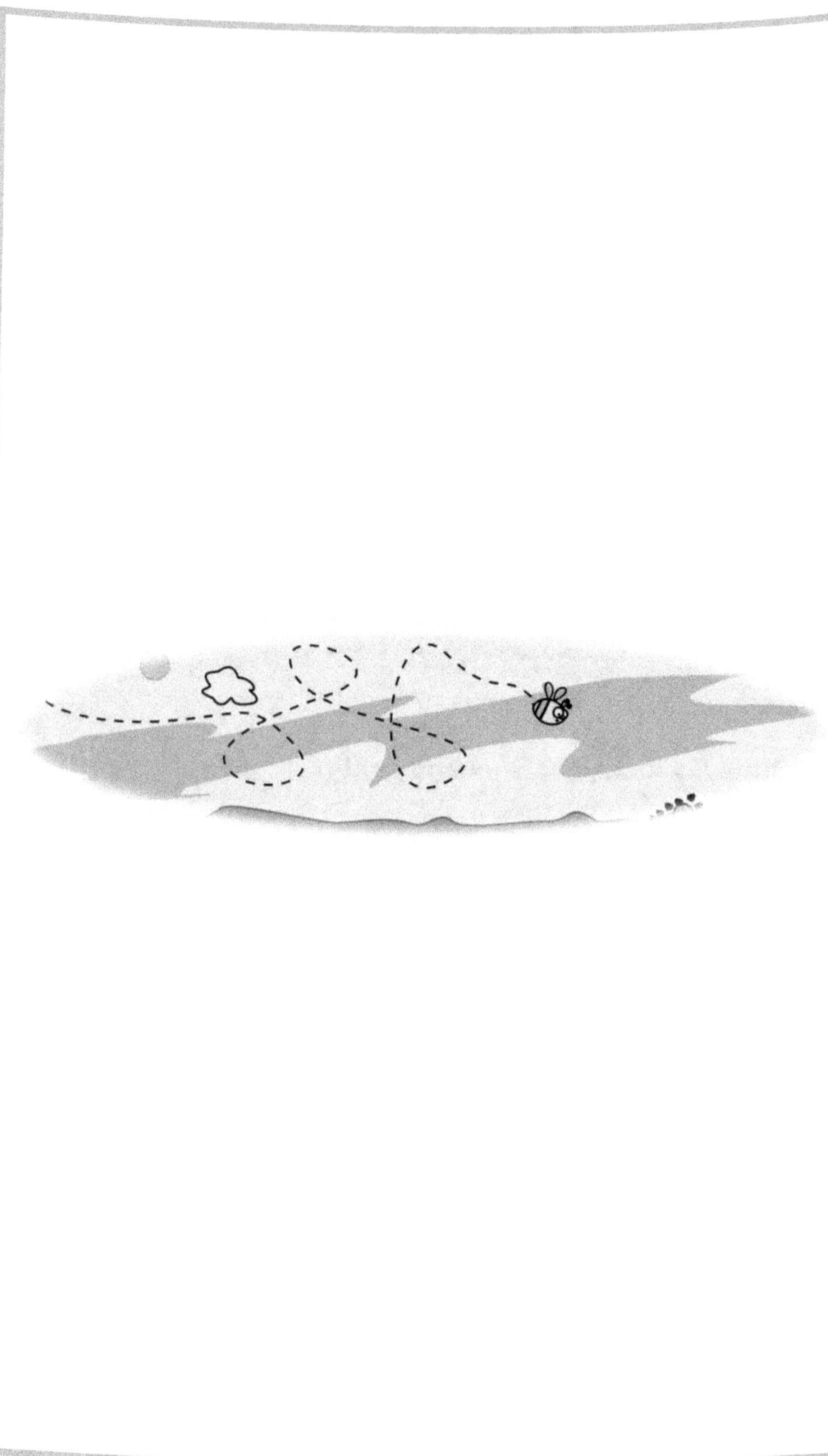

Boo replied-

Thank you Mr. Butterfly, that's very kind of you,
I will check with Roses if what you say is true.

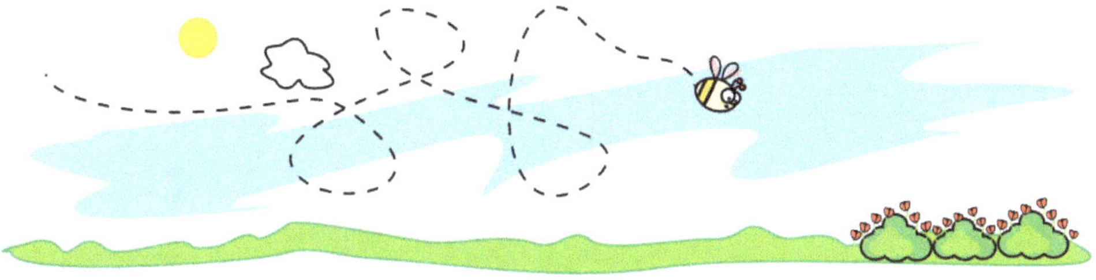

Up above and under little Boo flew,
To find if the Roses had really worn her shoe.

Boo flew down to the Roses, and asked-
Hello Mr. Red Rose, how do you do?
I am Boo, and I lost my shoe.

The Rose looked at Boo, and said-
Hello little Boo, and I see that too,
But about your shoe I have no clue.
My foot is in the ground, it's stuck like glue,
I know nothing about your shoe.

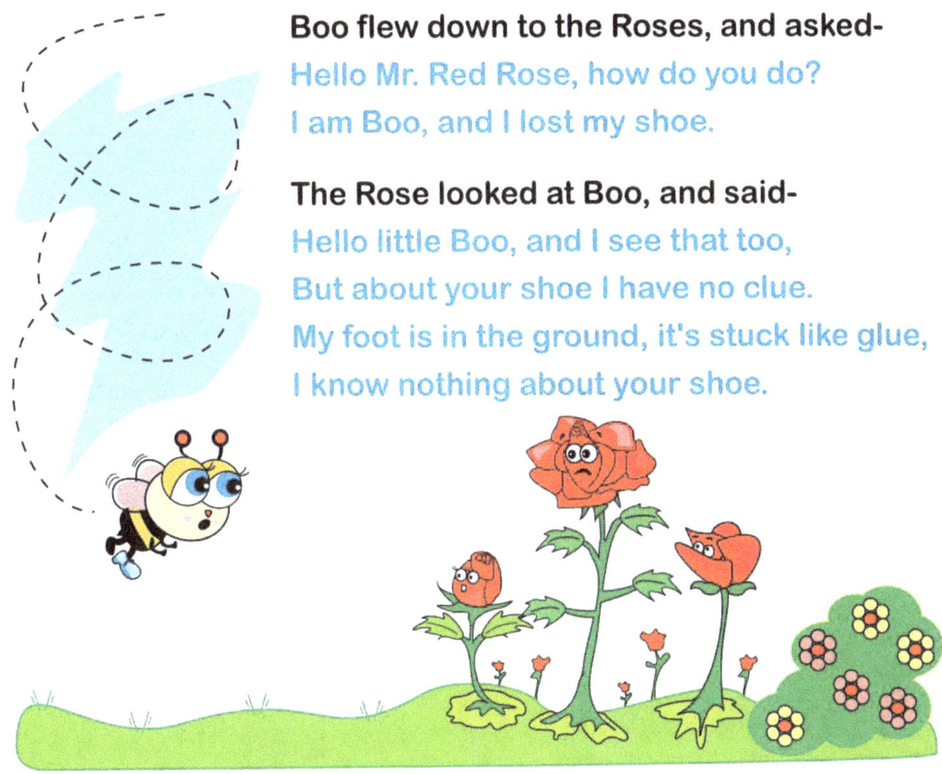

Little Boo looked at the Red Rose,
and then she looked at her one shoe;

AND THEN?

BOO, BOO, BOO,
cried little baby Boo,
BOO, BOO, BOO,
'I lost my shoe!'.

Hee
Haa
Huu

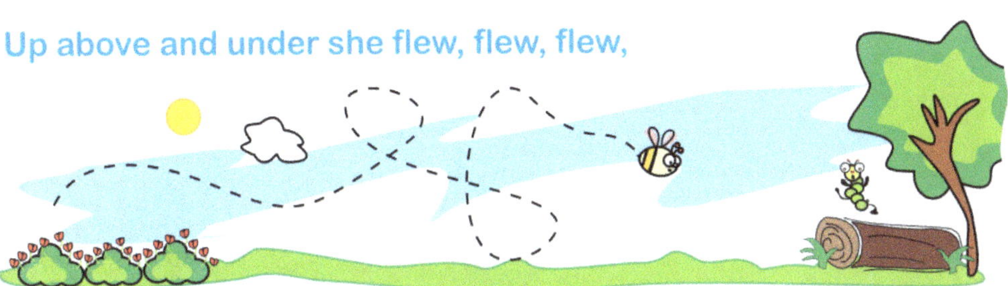

Up above and under she flew, flew, flew,

She saw a little Caterpillar doing Kung-Fu.

Boo flew down to the Caterpillar, and asked-
Hello Mr. Caterpillar, how do you do?
I am Boo, and I lost my shoe.
Oh! said the Caterpillar, I see that too,
I'll help you find it just follow my que.
Clue, Clue, Clue, let me look for a clue,
Who, who, who could have taken your shoe.

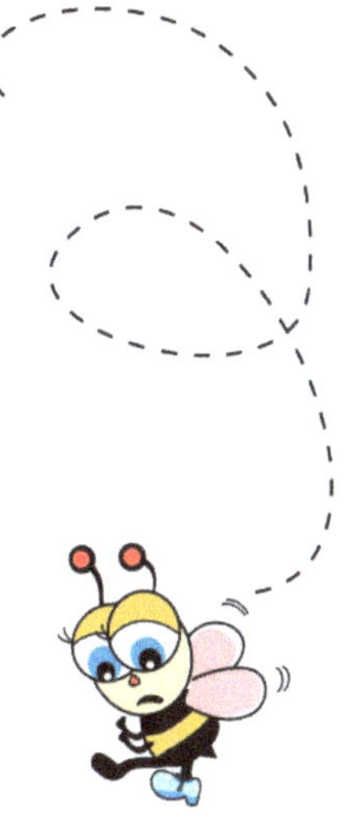

After an hour of walking around the caterpillar felt tired.
He said -

Hey little Boo I wish I knew,
But I can't find this shoe, shoe, shoe.
Go up this tree, and throw me that tissue,
As I feel like going to the Loo, Loo, Loo.

Little Boo looked at the tissue,
and then she looked at her one shoe,

AND THEN?

BOO, BOO, BOO,
cried little baby Boo,
BOO, BOO, BOO,
'I lost my shoe!'.

Up above and under she flew, flew, flew,
She saw a little Squirrel who was chewing cashew.

Boo flew down to the Squirrel, and asked-

Hello Mr. Squirrel, how are you?
I am Boo, and I lost my shoe.

Oh! said the Squirrel, I see that too,
Forget this shoe, and let's play peekaboo.

COO,
COO,

COO,
COO,

COO and
COO,

Come with me, and let's play peekaboo.

Little baby Boo looked at the Squirrel disappear,
and then she looked at her one shoe.

AND THEN?

BOO, BOO, BOO,
cried little baby Boo,
BOO, BOO, BOO,
'I lost my shoe!'.

Yawn!

Up above and under she flew, flew, flew,
She saw a fat Mouse who was eating his stew.

Boo flew down to the Mouse, and asked-

Hello Mr. Mouse, and what did you do?
It seems that your belly just grew, grew, grew.

'Shoo' said the little mouse, 'Shoo, Shoo, Shoo',
I just chewed a shoe that was blue, blue, blue.

Little Boo looked at the Mouse's tummy,
thinking of her one lost shoe.

AND THEN?

BOO, BOO, BOO, cried little baby Boo,
Oh! little mouse, you ate my shoe!

BOO, BOO, BOO, cried little baby Boo,
BOO, BOO, BOO, 'I lost my shoe'.

Tired and sad, little baby Boo lost all hope of finding her shoe.
She decided to fly back home with her one blue shoe.

As Boo entered the hive, Dew noticed the disappointed look
on her face. 'What happened my dear?' she asked,
'You look really upset.'

Boo sheepishly looked towards Dew. She was embarrassed
to let her mother know that she had lost one of her new shoes.
However, Boo felt it was important to tell her mother the truth.
She moved closer to Dew, and started narrating all that had
happened with her during the day.

Dew patiently heard all that Boo wanted to say.
She was happy to see the trust and courage Boo displayed
in telling her the truth. Boo was so tired that she slept while
talking. Dew quietly tucked Boo in her bed, and
kissed her good night as they went to sleep.

As the morning sun rose again, sparkling rays touched Boo's
tiny eyes waking her up. Boo opened her eyes, and was
surprised to see Dew sitting next to her bed.

Then all of a sudden, Boo jumped off her bed and screamed, 'Oh my god! Is this a dream?'. It was not a dream. She saw Dew holding both the 'Blue Shoes' in her hand.

Let's see what mommy Bee had to say-

Boo, Boo, Boo, Oh! my sweet little Boo,
You flew out yesterday, dropping one of two.

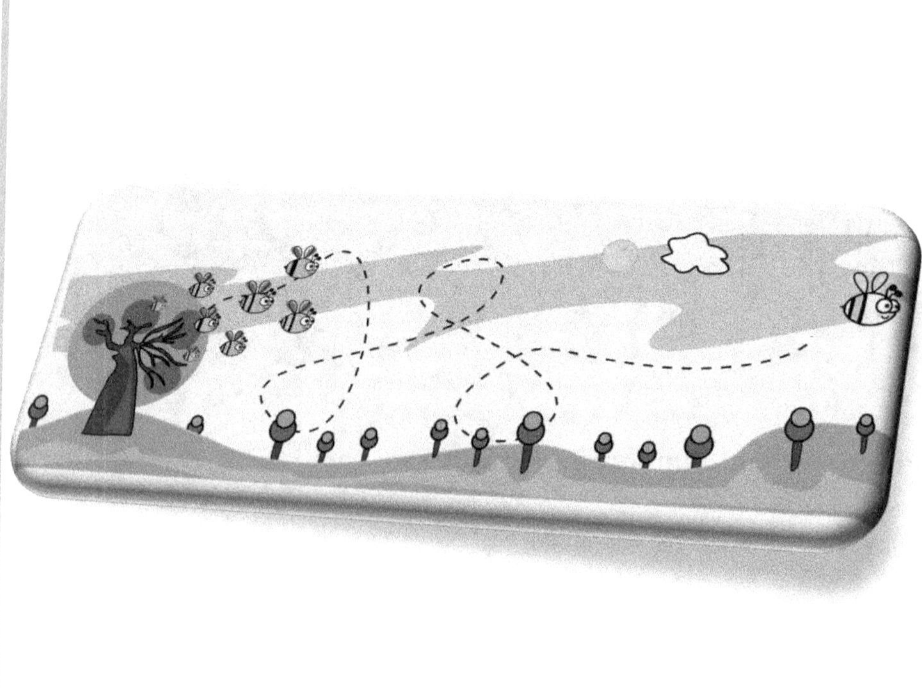

I sent the Bee's behind you like a crew, crew, crew;

But they lost you from their view as you flew, flew, flew.

My sweet little Boo you had never lost your shoe.

Little baby Boo looked at her Mother,
and then she looked at both her shoes.

She took both her shoes and wore them again.

AND THEN?

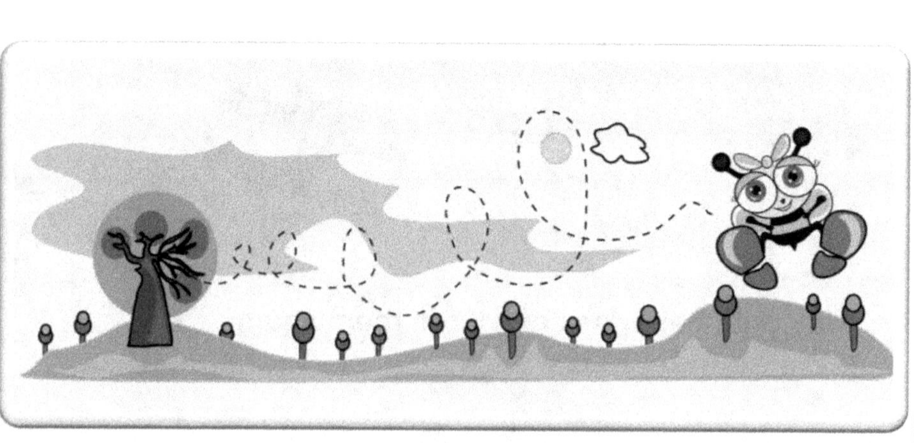

New, New, New, sang little baby Boo,
New, New, New, I found my shoe.

Up above and under she flew, flew, flew,
Little baby Boo had finally found her shoe.

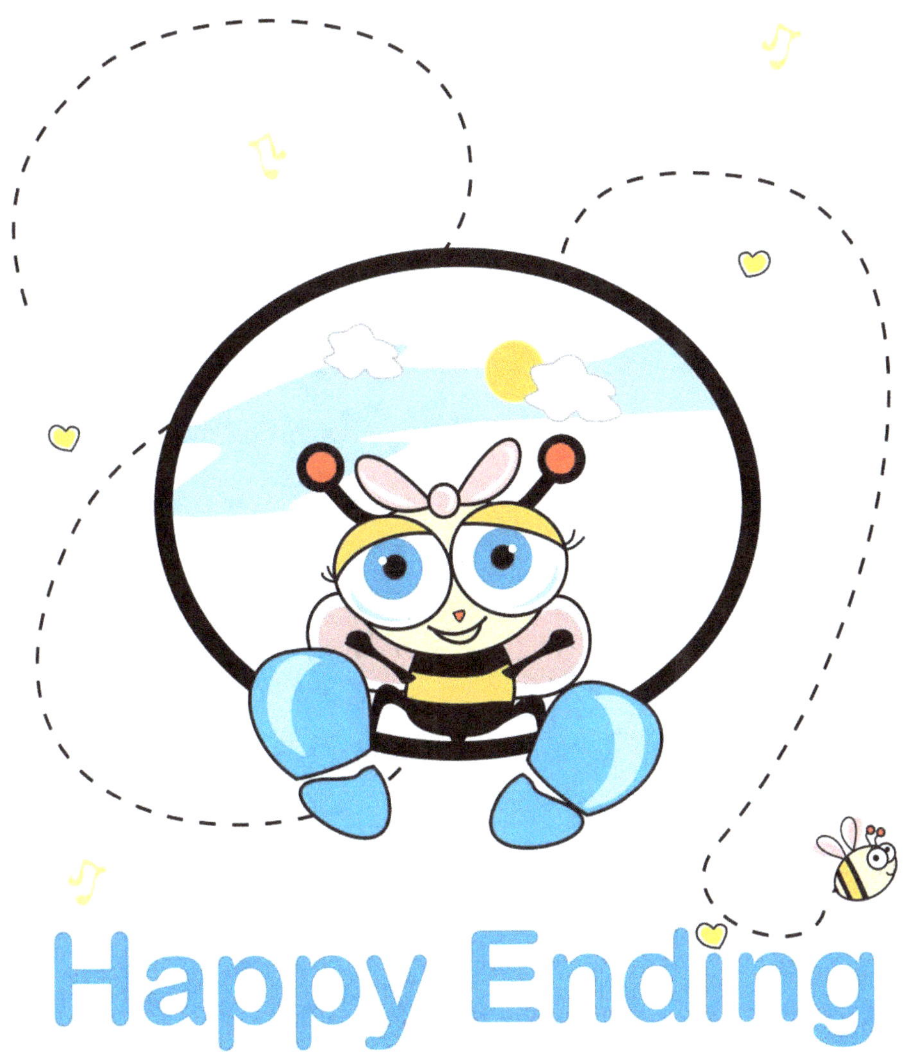

Happy Ending

My other children books on Kindle

Rhyme and Roll
An Illustrated Poem Book by- Shivohum

Monday Reading:
Happiness

Tuesday Reading
I Love the Moon

Wednesday Reading
I wish I could fly

Thursday Reading: Molly's Little Bud

Friday Reading:
The Mole Poem

Thankyou &
Happy Reading